POEMS

BY

AN OLD CODGER

Book Six

Final medley of rhyming
poetry on life and living
past and present

NEIL DAVIES

Illustration by Ben Tattersall (Grandson)

READERS' COMMENTS

- The number of poems written is truly wonderful, congratulations.

  K B Canada

- Joy to read.

  PW Bristol

- Congratulations, you're a poet as well as an old codger.

  G B London

- How talented you are.

  S R North Wales

- I laughed and I cried.

  M W Wrexham.

- What a wonderful poem …. the story of my life.

  M T Flint.

FOREWORD

In BOOK ONE I began with an apology for the way the world has become during my generation's failure to care for it.

BOOK SIX provides a concluding medley of rhyming poems, with a plea for international co-operation to deal with the world-wide evidence of global warning. I make no apology for expressing my concerns on life today within some of the poems. I am an old codger hoping that my pleas will not fall on deaf ears. Pass my message around by sharing this book, or better still, buy my books for your friends and family.

A few years ago, I set out to record, in print, reflections on my life over the 20th Century, hoping that in the years to come those that follow on will have some understanding of the significant developments in life and living that occurred during that era and are continuing almost daily.

It was the Greek statesman, Pericles, who said "What you leave behind is not what is engraved in stone monuments, but what is woven into the lives of others."

www.oldcodgersbook.co.uk

CONTENTS

OFF TO 'THE FRONT'

A crowded platform, a hissing train,
An air of emotion and mutual strain.
Men and boys in their new military gear,
Await orders to board, masking their fear.

A one-way ticket up to the Front,
This journey is no Hollywood Stunt.
Green countryside passes by,
A pleasant land betrays 'The Lie'.

Disembarked to noise and cordite air,
Stretcher bearers pass, bodies with eyes that stare.
They said, "It will all be over by Christmastide",
But battlefields churned up mud, so far and wide.

Their military gear no longer new,
Socks and boots all sodden through.
Trenches open to all weather and shell,
This 'Front' is just a living hell.

The 'Front' back and forth, across the terrain,
As battles continue to wax and wane.
Scrambling up and over the top,
Oh! when will this carnage ever stop.

Wives and mothers, seeking mutual solace,
Waiting for news but fearing the worse.
A dining table set place, an empty chair,
Dreading that telegram, a house of despair.

Eight million dead, twenty-one million wounded alas,
From artillery, small arms, and poison gas.
Trench warfare witnessed at its worse,
A challenge for any field doctor or nurse.

'A war to end all wars' they said in vain,
Twenty-one years later, all over again.
A world-wide conflict, more loss, more pain,
Near Eighty-Five million; it's quite insane! **

From early times man has sought to gain
More land, its minerals, and all the terrain,
By violence and fear and evil intent,
Seeking power and dominance, never content.

By leaders who cannot live in peace or harmony,
Their lives are full of animosity and acrimony.
Achieving their goal by violence and felony,
Creating international mayhem and instability

/over

Is the pen mightier than the sword?
Not empty words uttered by every evil warlord.
Empty promises now strike many a chord,
As we remember those that lie in graves abroad.

** Up to 85 million perished world-wide.
55 million in conflict – military and civilian.
25 million war-related, disease and famine.
UK: 450,000 military and civilian. (380,000 killed)
From the end of WW2 up to the end of the 20th Century
over 300 wars and civil conflicts have taken place. Wikipedia.

000 - 000

A ROSE IS LIKE A MOTHER

A rose is like a mother,
A comparison there is no other.
Petals of protection encircling the heart,
Layer after layer right from the start.

The beauty of a rose in bloom
It's scent enveloping every room,
Reflects a mother's life of love and care,
Her generosity for all to share.

Rootstock of a rose gives hardness and stability,
A mother's strength is rooted in her ancestry.
A flowering stem growing upright and strong,
A growing child taught right from wrong.

Thorns of protection keep danger at bay,
Like words of guidance that mothers say.
As roses stretch to face the sun,
Mothers reach out a hand to daughter or son.

As time goes by the petals will fall,
It is an era that comes to one and all.
Bottle the perfume to hold the memory,
Store those words, for it's your mother's story.

000 - 000

HANDS

Hands that greet
When people you meet,
At the door
Or on the street.

Hands that care,
Hands that stroke,
Hands that wash
And brush your hair.

Hands that stir,
Hands that cook.
Hands that hold
Your favourite book.

Hands that clap
In appreciation,
Recognition.
To musical notation.

Hands that caress
And hold you close,
When life throws a curveball
And causes stress.

Hands that draw,
Hands that paint.
Hands that hold you
When you are feeling faint.

Hands that knit,
Hands that sew,
Hands that tie,
And reach up to the sky.

Hands that dig,
Or hold a 'cig'.
That talk with feeling,
To the deaf and hard of hearing.

Hands that show your age,
And your matrimonial stage.
An indicator of your health,
Your life revealed on this human page.

Hands that help make beautiful sounds,
Hands that create a dreadful noise.
Musical instruments in harmony,
Or a toddler with his or her toy.

Hands that come together,
In silent prayer or meditation.
An act of grateful thanks,
Or one of humble benediction.

Hands are creators, receivers, givers,
Hands that help and support others.
Hands that tightly held their mothers,
Hands that hold forever lovers.

000 - 000

A DAY IN THE LIFE AT No 8

Morning breakfast made for me,
All washed down with a mug of tea.
A garden stroll, a place to sit,
Check if badger Butin's paid a visit.

A tasty lunch of regular variety,
'Bargain Hunt' and news on TV.
An involuntary nap, I've missed the lot,
Was the weather forecast cold or hot?

Clear my emails, deleting many,
I'd be a rich man if, for each, I had a penny.
A tea break declared at the stroke of Three,
With a debrief on the world by her and me.

The lass has done the washing, made the bed,
Another active day it has to be said.
Ponders on the forthcoming meal of the day,
And invites me now to have a say.

Alas, I've no idea what's in the freezer,
For this decrepit, old, worn out, geezer.
Fish or chicken, liver, or ham,
Any response would be a sham.

A decision is agreed, Ah! Then it's changed!
Sell-by-date demands meal plan be re-arranged!
The versatility of this dear old lass,
Is akin to a magician nationally hailed 'first class'.

The kitchen isn't large, nor is it small,
But one cook has to do it all.
This old codger is obliged to check the wine,
Condiments, cutlery, and the table laid out fine.

Another meal of great delight,
Not a morsal left in sight.
We've a machine, top of the range,
I load it up, she arrives to rearrange!

A decaf tea for evening 'compline',
A shut down of all things live and on-line.
A check around to keep us safe and sound,
You never know who's prowling around.

A quick review of this epistle is revealing,
Imbalance of our internal domestic job sharing.
In litigation, external jobs are ever demanding,
So, it's a matter of mutual understanding.

000 – 000

WHAT IS LOVE? (2)

Sitting on the grassy bower,
Plucking out the petals of the daisy flower.
She asked the question, her heart in a knot,
'Loves me, loves me not'?

Played by maids from Victorian days,
Seeking an answer by childhood ways.
The last petal to seal their fate,
Enchanting, amusing, but never accurate.

A fortune teller's crystal revealing all,
The answers from a cylindrical glass ball.
A pack of cards spread out to reveal the truth,
Finding out about love from a mystical sleuth.

Forget the daisies, tarot cards, fortune tellers,
Fancy hair, coloured nails, chat room fellas.
Artificial, superficial, body images
Found on many magazine pages.

Don't go searching with false enhancement,
Don't deceive, stay honest and transparent.
Visual beauty is subjective and temporary,
Beauty is in the heart, the soul, the memory.

Be alive to all around you, he'll be waiting,
A chance encounter, an emotional feeling.
You will know that he's the one,
A moment when togetherness feels like fun.

RAIN

"It rained on Monday,
And it rained on Tuesday,
And rained on Wednesday too.
It rained on Thursday,
And it rained on Friday,
And it rained all Saturday through.
Along came Sunday,
and I thought that's one day
when it certainly won't rain.
But it poured all Sunday,
And along came Monday,
And it started all over again."

The words of a song I learned as a lad,
I never thought that it would be that bad.
But I sit here now as rain lashes down,
As it is in every village, city, and town.

The earth's in distress across our seas and 'scapes,
With floods and fires, famine and 'quakes.
And man is turning on man wherever they stand,
The desecration of flesh, of homes and land.

This fragile world is going off balance,
To correct our errors do we have a chance?
A failing planet due to human action,
A scientific health check has produced a reaction. *

/over

Nine planetary boundaries for habitable existence
From climate change to freshwater supply,
Atmospheric pollution, ozone depletion, to chemical
dispense
Six have been crossed; to recover we all
must now comply.

*Stockholm Resilience Centre.

000 - 000

FATHERHOOD

This is a task not all can manage,
The responsibility a life-time challenge.

The outcome can be quite rewarding
To watch your children grow up strong,
Understanding right from wrong,
Developing a mutual bond so strong.

A child needs a father to hold his or her hand,
Help walk safe through life's challenging land.
To call on for guidance, support, advice,
One who does not have to be asked twice.

Absence from the family life,
Through work or duty, or family strife,
Can leave a hole, a damaged soul.
But tender care can help restore.

A lifetime duty but a life-long pleasure,
A helping hand keeps their life secure.
Be there when life gets tough,
When dark clouds threaten, and seas are rough.

It's a job for life with no pension,
Hours of pleasure, sometimes tension.
No monitory gain, no retirement pay,
But the reward is before you every day.

/over

As Charles Kettering suggested long ago

"Every father should remember one day his son will follow his example not his advice."

Howard W Hunter

"One of the greatest things a father can do for his children is to love their mother."

,

000 - 000

SOLVING ONE, CREATING TWO

I've said it before,
I'll say it again.
Solving one problem may be the aim,
But begats another or even more pain.

When heat was created by burning coal
And steam was harnessed for control,
Technology, travel, all acclaimed with pride,
Then its pollution spread far and wide.

Scientist introduced us to plasticity,
With its many properties and adaptability.
Plastic has dominated our life everywhere,
But poisoned our lands, our seas, and air.

Experimental bugs in a Far Eastern continent,
Escaped and caused mayhem wherever it went.
Trying to solve a problem without due care,
Caused human suffering in every thoroughfare.

No war has ever achieved total peace,
More bitter conflicts have been released.
The arrow replaced by guns large and small,
Cannon balls by shells, full of poison, released to fall.

/over

Atomic bombs to nuclear fusion,
Missiles unmanned causing public confusion.
Wars in a field far from home,
Are now all fought on streets where we roam.

We've lost control of the World Wide Web,
Moved too slow it must be said.
Opportunities to improve our life and living,
Communicate, educate, so groundbreaking.

Failing to achieve such an accomplishment,
Highjacked by those with evil intent.
People of all ages now wary of going online,
This international 'solution' has lost its shine.

000 - 000

GRATEFUL THANKS TO ALL MOTHERS AT CHRISTMASTIDE

Christmases come, Christmases go,
We've witnessed them all since long ago.
Warm sunny days, deep, deep, snow,
Clear blue skies, dark clouds hanging low.

Christmas trees standing over family presents,
Dolls and annuals, scarves, and scents.
Cycles and pedal cars for outside fun,
All unwrapped before breakfast had begun.

Santa's drink and mince all gone,
Rudolph's carrot devoured 'in one'.
Tipped upstairs in the dead of night,
Stockings full, left not quite out of sight.

Washed and peeled, chopped, and scraped,
I'm sure your bodies must have ached.
Filled the bird with home-made stuffing,
Never considered Yorkshire Pudding!

Hours of shopping to fill the table,
Planning and preparation quite considerable.
The food laid out with stuffing and sprout,
'Dinner's ready' comes the annual shout.

/over

A well-thumbed book of friends no longer,
But friendship memories are ever stronger.
Christmas cards now go in a new direction,
To our growing family with affection.

Exhaustion is a word that comes to mind,
Annual endurance of the Christmas Grind.
It took you up to New Year to unwind,
You never complained, you've been so kind.

So, thank you all for the years past,
I'm sure that this will not be the last.
Ignore the hype, the constant chatter,
Next year, let's just have chips and fish in batter.

000 - 000

OLD AGE

"We should all be born old and grow young",
so said my mother.

A rather odd comment to make,
But I've given it a second take.
Deeply into old age and needing support,
I understand now why she uttered that thought.

If you live long enough and friends have all gone,
Years of experience, knowledge and skill, are as none.
Mental and physical capacity is on the wane,
You know what to do, but can't, it's a shame.

'Too old lad, you need someone younger,
Knows how to solder and use a sink plunger.
Good with a spade and when to prune roses,
Water the gardens with no kinks in the hoses.'

'Can bend very low and climb up a ladder,
Work many hours, has a good bladder.
Knows all the tools and tricks of the trade,'
'I'll be back' is the call when he's finally paid.

/over

Living longer in a fast-moving world,
Not knowing what's about to unfold.
Time to ponder, to look back, reminisce,
Prompted my mother to ponder
on what she may have missed.

So, never say NO, grab every chance
At work and play, even romance.
Keep up the pace, but never a race,
And enjoy a life full of kindness and grace.

000 - 000

GLOBAL WARNING

Challenges ahead to recover our planet,

Life and living are under threat.

Industrial revolution to plastic technology,

Man-made pollution now a climate emergency.

Average temperature rising more rapid than ever,

Trapping more heat causing global terror.

El Nino's around affecting our weather.

Carbon fuels will have to go,

Heating, driving, by fossil fuels, held low.

Adapt the wind, sea, sun and more,

Nuclear energy for peaceful power.

Gather evidence of each nation's remedial action,

Eliminate the causes of this global reaction

I NEVER THOUGHT

I never thought that I would witness
Doctors, teachers in fancy dress,
With Flowerpot Hats and sheets of cardboard
Like sheep on the side of a public road.

In desperation and frustration,
Professional folk have taken action.
Overwhelmed by patient numbers,
Undervalued by politician, but not the nation.

Likewise breaks in classroom tuition,
On top of COVID across the nation.
Progressive learning has been lost,
We are yet to know the full effect and cost.

Their mentors forced to forsake role and position,
Standing not in their classroom but roadside location.
Classroom recovery will take a generation,
Teenagers ill prepared to later lead our nation

Alas, the need to strike is the final action,
A call to the nation of their situation.
Overworked, under resourced, confused,
Public workers are all being abused.

A call for more money is a lost fight,
Such high expectations are out of sight.
The public purse has leaked away,
Political minds long been in decay.

Near three trillion is our National Debt,
Plus interest charges we can't forget.
It's time to put our shoulder to the plough,
The Government needs to tell us where and how.

000 - 000

VARIETY

"There was a very cautious man
Who never romped nor played.
He never laughed nor ever dreamed,
Nor kissed a pretty maid.
,

And when he passed away, they say
insurance was denied.
Since he'd never really lived,
*They claimed he never died." ***

. . . .

Variety is the spice of life,
That gives it all its flavour. **

Particularly at a time of world-wide strife,
For many, a possible saviour.

Sameness, conformity, familiarity,
And a life of daily monotony,
Numb the senses, shorten horizons.
Are forms of insidious mental poisons.

Life and living can be restraining,
Choice and liberty undermining.
Recognise this proverbial quotation,
Variety can be diversity, choice, planned rotation.

Change the menu of your day,
A new sport that you can play.
Vary your route to work each day,
Or plan your next year's holiday.

Variety theatre is a mix of entertainment,
Takes one away from the daily commitment.
Another world of fact and fiction,
A laugh, a song, a trigger of emotion.

Choice is a tool of variety,
But beware it does not cause anxiety.
Diversity another quality to embrace,
A natural occurrence in the human race.

Embrace variety, create variety,
Throughout your life build up a medley.
A potpourri of the colours in your memory,
And those many flavours of your life story.

There's nothing new in this rhyming ditty,
It's all about having the opportunity,
And encouragement, support, and one's tenacity.
But remember, variety of life can be free.

*Unknown

**"The Task" by William Cowper (1731-1800)

000 - 000

AN UNUSUAL HOME DELIVERY

It is more than three score years and ten,
When I first met a remarkable chicken hen.
At the bottom of our garden she resided,
With a small flock but she was single minded.

This Rhode Island Red had personality,
Independent lady, determined, no frivolity.
We called her "Cheeky" as you will see,
But not the sort to sit on your knee.

When nature called, she sought a warm nest,
Some used the egg-laying booth to come to rest.
But this young lady had none of that,
Desiring the comfort of a centrally heated 'flat'.

She had the audacity to come a'calling,
Her behaviour was quite appalling.
This flighty lass would fly on to the windowsill.
And tap the glass which took some skill.

"Cheeky" was demanding we open our back door,
She had begun to walk in, our daily transgressor.
To see if we had a suitable place to lay,
It was happening here every day.

She was a lady of some finesse,
Not going to lay on some old grassy garden mess.
In she would walk with grace and style,
Discovered the space where she could spend a while.

She would enter our kitchen and turn left, **
Into the bathroom, assured of no damage nor theft.
On the floor behind the bath, she sat to lay,
On the waiting clothes to wash on the next dry day.

With a proud 'cluck' up she would rise,
Passing by as she left us the prize.
And strolled away with pride and candour,
Back into the garden through the open door.

She was almost human in many ways,
Such friendship, such trust, really pays.
How could you eat a chicken like that,
When the time comes to add a touch of fat.

** See 'Step Changes' poem in Book One

000 - 000

NATURE UNDER THREAT

On mountains high and valleys deep,
Wild ponies roam among hardy sheep.
Spanning thousands of years quietly foraging,
On hillsides, grasslands, all thanks to hefting.

Birds of prey fly above ruling the sky,
Raptors circling before down they dive.
Buzzards, kites, hawks, and harriers so shy,
A vulnerable target has caught their eye.

Mountain streams meander down to valley floor,
Filling lakes for urban fresh water store.
Lush meadows full of wild flowers and bees,
Butterflies, moths, and tall proud trees.

Ground nesting birds defying predatory foes,
Camouflaged within grasses and shallow shoals.
Curlews, snipes, lapwings, nightjar,
Blending seamlessly within the flora.

Man has developed things that destroy
Not only life but what we enjoy.
Scarring mountainsides, poisoning our air
Where nature has long maintained its care.

Our Mount Eryri* has been raped by man,
Someone had a devious plan.
A tourist attraction, for all and sundry,
They're coming here from every country.

A leisure park with narrow gauge train,
Just to help take up the strain.
Avoiding any next day's aches,
Arrive at the top for tea and cakes.

Six different paths to choose your way,
Littered highways, era of our 'throw away'.
To hell with the habitat and countryside,
From national nature reserve to barren hillside.

*Snowdon

000 - 000

MURDER ON THE LAWN

There's been a murder on the lawn,
The whole garden now looks quite forlorn.
The act was so swift, so silent,
Clearly a killing quite brutal and violent.

As we sat with our cake and tea,
A murderous act not nice to see
Was occurring just metres away,
An innocent victim's final day.

The evidence is scattered everywhere,
But no body to offer burial care.
Victim's remains have been removed,
Attacker carried them off, that's clearly proved.

Evidence gathered, statements taken,
Not the first time this has happened.
Same spot, same time of day,
But body remains then left to decay.

A dark covered suspect with a clear hook nose,
Had been sighted standing quite close
The day before, as still as a brick,
His presence and posture we did not click.

The lawn is scattered with white breast down,
Soft and curly, tufts of plumage all around.
Facts are gathered, the evidence is full,
Our sparrow hawk has taken another pigeon or gull.

This is nature from time long ago,
When survival requires behaviour so low.
When humans act in a similar way,
They must be made to pay.

Some are ill, some are evil,
Cold and callous, on drug or pill
Life-long incarceration for safety's sake
Early diagnosis with no mistake.

000 - 000

OUR GARDEN VISITOR.

MY MORNING SAGA

Digesting my meal of porridge in a bag,
Whilst also digesting my Kindle's daily 'rag',
The news is all just gloom and alarm
Of Leaders who have neither brain, nor charm.

The world is on fire as the scriptures said,
I'll have to build a heat-proof shed.
Take in creatures two by two,
With just room for me and you.

No phones, no emails, no internet,
No cinema, no one-stop market.
The sea will boil and cook the fish,
Cod on toast will be our daily dish.

It's all too much to comprehend,
Daily news sends me round the bend.
So, let's stay cool and cut our emissions,
Eradicate the gases by ALL the nations.

/over

It's too serious to play this game,
Time is short to seek out blame.
The evidence is clear for all to see,
To talk and dither would be a tragedy.

Then each morning I can munch and crunch,
And later enjoy my lunchtime brunch.
All will be well with our fragile earth,
A planet with a future, a new clean birth.

000 - 000

OUR INDUSTRIAL REVOLUTION
CAME LATER

A medieval hamlet, the odd farm, occasional hedge,
From Roman settlement to the Alyn valley edge.
A peaceful scene, years of sun and snow,
With rich seams of coal undisturbed down below.

This hamlet was part of a nearby community,
No church, no separate identity.
Later given the name of Llay, Welsh for meadow*
Where cattle graze and wild flowers grow.

Bersham ironworks in the industrial revolution,
Made cannon balls to achieve a Civil War solution.
Brymbo steel works going full blast,
How long did those local industries last.

Nearby mines worked by men with shovel and pick,
But output was often low and, sadly, work sporadic.
The 20th Century arrived and World War One broke out,
The demand for coal was the loudest shout.

The local area reflected the industrial revolution,
But this old hamlet remained a peaceful bastion.
Until a geological survey revealed to all,
Down below rich seams of high-class coal.

/over

As World War One battled on in France,
The hamlet lost its country romance.
Miners from far and near arrived with families,
Arrangements made to meet their needs.

Housed in huts they set to work,
To reach this coal they did not shirk.
The mine owners also played their part,
Creating a model village with a beating heart.

Electricity fed from the mine to every building,
Church and chapels, and school for learning.
The largest workforce of any mine in Wales,
Two thousand five hundred men and boys, no females

Deepest pit in the country, over three thousand feet,
Miners sweating in the dust and heat.
Output peaked at a million tons in 'Twenty-Nine,
Highest output of coal for any mine.

Now in the throes of a local industrial revolution,
The village faced subsidence and pollution.
A price to pay to heat the nation,
The hamlet lost in this model village creation.

*Llai

000 - 000

IT'S A BOY!

A celebration, the birth of a child,
Family and friends are totally beguiled.
The miracle of creation no greater event,
A baby boy, so pure, so innocent.

A mop of hair and big round eyes,
He utters a cry, the midwife sighs.
Quickly enshrined in a fresh clean towel,
Laid on the scales, was that a scowl?

Eyes that yet to fully see,
To smile or sit on his mother's knee.
To learn of all the wonderous things,
That life and love and friendship brings.

To see the sky, the sun, the sea,
A flower, the grass, a bumble bee.
A bus, a train, an aeroplane,
The moon and stars and showers of rain.

A dancing shadow, a mirror's reflection,
So many things he'll want to question.
What lies ahead for this dear young soul,
And for his new compatriots all.

/over

Perhaps a statesman, or peace maker,
Perhaps a butcher or a baker.
What is the future for this little star?
*What will be, will be, Que Sera, Sera**

*Doris Day's signature song from the Alfred Hitchcock's film
'The Man Who Knew Too Much', 1956.

For my grandsons and great grandsons.

000 - 000

WAR ON MY DOORSTEP

I've just witnessed a violent act,
Outside my window and that's a fact.
Aggression, bullying and headbutting too,
In daylight here, at half past two.

Mob rule is taking place, blow after blow,
A crowd is gathering ready to have a go.
As one drops down onto the floor,
Another, steps in to settle a score.

Two little sparrows sitting on the fence,
Spotted the feeder with its fat ball contents.
Quickly they landed and shared the space,
Alas, more birds approached at a hell of a pace.

They came like a war-time Kamikaze attack,
Trying to land on front, sides and back.
Frantic action towards one another,
Beaks and wings weapons of potential murder.

Attacking each other, the feeder swaying 'to and fro',
The bullies not aware of the fat crumbs on the floor.
The young sought the hedge to escape the hate,
The wise enjoying the pickings down 'on a plate'.

Aggression is a one-dimensional act,
To destroy all around with little tact.
No consideration, no perception,
No sensitivity nor discretion.
Does this sound familiar?

HOME AIDS

I have a small white plastic clock,
A silent time piece, no tick, no tock.
Tripple As provide the power and light,
It's timekeeping controlled by a satellite.

When British time goes back and to,
Twice a year at night, at two.
This little clock is adjusting while I sleep,
By a satellite signal, it's quite neat.

There's 450 Time pieces at Windsor Castle,
What a lot of twice-year hassle,
And all the others in the priceless Royal Collection.
Ah! If only they had satellite clock synchronisation.

Then there's Alexa, at attention night and day,
Is she listening to what we have to say?
Can this be Big Brother 1984*come true,
Or a valuable home aid for me and you.

She understands whatever we ask,
So polite as she carries out every task.
A vocal encyclopaedia, Wikipedia with sound,
Music 'on call' for all tastes, it's quite profound.

Looking back as old codgers tend to do,
Aids in our homes were very few.
Hot water on tap was not for all,
Illumination by gas mantles on the wall.

It was constant daily toil and strife,
And so, for many a miserable life.
Domestic slog, no manicures,
Little comfort, simple pleasures.

When collieries were taken over by the NCB, **
Improved conditions, regular weekly money.
Gradually life and living would be changed,
Offering domestic goods across the range.

Television aerials strapped to every chimney,
TVs providing daily news, dramas, comedy.
Sporting events initially in black and white,
Electricity for heating and tungsten light.

Salesmen called to sell their carpet cleaners,
Brushes, clothes, encyclopaedias,
Shops sold electric kettles, irons, and toasters,
And coal miners soon became keen car roadsters.

/over

Today, washing machines that will also dry,
Dishwashers cleaning pots, so pleasing to the eye.
Microwave ovens, new forms of cooking,
Electric hair dryers that can assist with styling.

I've witnessed the greatest rate of change
Of life and living of any age.
Science and technology have removed the drudgery,
Eliminating the misery of kitchen slavery.

*George Orwell's novel 1984

**National Coal Board

000 - 000

NOT GOING OUT DRESSED LIKE THAT

You're not going out dressed like that,
Your shirt needs washing and ironing flat.

You're not going out dressed like that,
The pattern makes you look old and fat.

You're not going out dressed like that,
Your jacket can now accommodate two for a chat.

You're not going out dressed like that,
Your flat cap looks like an old skinned rat.

This old codger has reached an age,
Where comfort over-rules the fashion page.
But our young are subject to fashion imagery,
Beyond a level of common decency.

You're not going out dressed like that,
The hem's too short and that's a fact.

You're not going out dressed like that,
It's cold, you need your coat and hat.

You're not going out dressed like that,
Just sit down here we need to chat.

/over

'You're not going out dressed like that',
How many parents have armed for combat,
As they prepare for an adolescent domestic fray.
But we all know fashion of the day does not stay.

It's that period of experimentation,
An element of teenage elation.
Freedom to put a toe in the modern world,
Independence from always being told.

'You're not going out dressed like that!'
And that's final.

000 - 000

MY GENETIC CODE 1

Who am I, this old codger I see,
Do I have a good pedigree.
Or does a mongrel strain lie within,
A scattering of evil thoughts and sin.

Were my forebearers victims of plight or situation,
Taken advantage of by those of rank and position.
Full of bad intent and lust,
Or were they upstanding that one could trust.

My DNA reveals my origin of long ago,
But who was responsible for my nose and big toe.
I've acquired a past-down family story,
Throwing a light on my maternal history.

A story of love from adversity,
A gesture of kindness and charity.
My great grandmother a foundling bairn,
Lying in a blanket on a small roadside cairn.

Near Ruthin, the old county castle fort,
Named from its red sandstone support.
It was around 1850 and there laid a human pearl,
When John Parry found this new born girl.

On a road along the Clwydian Range
This road sweeper saw something strange.
He swept her up onto his chest,
Carried her home for food, warmth, and rest.

/over

John and his wife gave her a Welsh name
for recognition,
They called her Winifred, *blessed reconciliation.*
But who was her mum, who was her dad?
Her situation was very sad.

Ten miles west as the crow might travel,
In the gap of the Clwydian hills.
The village of Bodfari lies,
With Offa's Dyke it has strong ties.

An overnight stop for any keen walker,
Saint Winifred of Holywell's healing water,
Our Seventh Century virgin martyr,
Called to see the Welsh recluse called Deifer.

It was here a baby boy was born,
Around 1850 too, but he was not alone.
With two brothers and five sisters,
He was named Morgan Salisbury Jones.

Some years later fate came into play,
When Winifred grew up and moved away.
To work and live with the Bather family,
In Denbigh town quite close to old Bodfari.

She took the Bather name when she came to marry
Morgan Salisbury Jones at the Church of St Hilary.
One of their children was John Robert Jones, my Taid,
Gresford colliery is where he worked and where he died.

....
.

Then, there's my other maternal great, great, gran,
An illegitimate child named Ann.
A strong personality with an odd-shaped nose,
Liked to dress in men's leather clothes.

But that's a story for a later page.

000 - 000

Winifred with son her Tom (Taid's brother)

Poetry is the one place where people

can speak their original human mind.

It is the outlet for people to say in public

What is known in private.

Allen Grinsberg.

1926 - 1997

NINE MEN DIE EVERY YEAR!

Nine men die every year,
So I'm warned by my old dear.
From what ailment could it be,
Is it too many cups of black coffee?

Is it from drinking too much beer?
Or wearing too tight undergear.
I have been feeling rather queer,
I shall wait to see if spots appear.

Have those guys young or old,
Not behaved as they were told.
Ignoring health and safety codes,
Or fast traffic on our crowded roads.

Did they strain their hearts too much,
Living their lives in a constant rush.
Or sat around, lazy, and getting fat,
All day sleeping on their exercise mat.

What has caused these men to fall,
Every year some short, some tall.
Is the answer in this final verse I wonder,
Time to reveal, no longer ponder.

The answer lies on the final leaf *
It really is beyond belief
Are you heading to join the nine,
Or have I saved you just in time.
***Please go to the end of the book.**

(By the author)

Acton Park.

Home of the

TREE OF THE YEAR 2023

Four poems forward in this book.

MOTORISTS UNDER ATTACK AGAIN

Driving along our urban street,
Beware what hazards you may meet.
Pot holes to the left, pot holes to the right,
An expensive car repair bill is in sight.

Driving along our urban street,
Beware when parents and pupils meet.
Resist your trip when out of school they pour,
Highway Code and Kerb Drill they just ignore.

Driving along our urban street,
For work, deliveries, to shop, or to eat.
Lamp posts either side standing tall,
A 'guard of honour'? No, they are a warning call.

Driving along our urban street,
New signs to warn, not to greet.
It's twenty miles per hour, we all must obey,
The Senedd guys have had their way.

Forget your heated seats to warm your pores,
Self-parking, and keyless doors.
Enjoy the scenery as you trundle by,
Slow enough to count those street lights up so high.

What was wrong with those protected places,
With cameras placed to record in those spaces.
Are our streets now to be camera littered,
Taxpayers' money again to be frittered.

It's second gear all the way,
Extra fuel means more to pay.
A price to pay for saving lives,
If only our streets were clear of knives.

. . . .

p.s. Road accidents are not a new event,
Since man walked in front waving a pennant.
Every driver on a road, everyone near a road
Needs to be vigilant, self-protection is your code.

000 - 000

"I DON'T BELIEVE IT!"

The words of Victor Meldrew* on many an occasion,
On TV screens across the nation.
Modern life upsetting his suburban comfort.
Can you believe my reflective automotive report?

The growth of transport by internal combustion,
A time when all cars had a colour option.
Black, or for second-hand option, black and rust,
Bought from a local garage you could trust.

Behind the wheel, having passed 'The Test',
There's a box of gears in their oily nest.
Two pedals to engage and move, and one to stop,
A handbrake to park or emergency backstop.

But that was not all, once you are on the road,
Cars in front and behind, lorries with their heavy load.
To turn right ahead a sequence had to be followed,
Wind down the window, right arm fully extended.

Gather it back in to help turn the wheel when traffic
allows,
Never mind their horns as the traffic behind grows.
But turning left ahead required unusual physical motion,
Wind down the window, right arm goes into rotation.

Gather it back in to turn left and then drive on ahead,
All this whilst selecting the right gears in their oily bed.
If it's raining, there are more gymnastics
but not so grand,
Vacuum powered windscreen wipers
Or switched on and off by hand.

No warning lights when brakes were applied,
Planned action required to signal intention
for those behind.
Wind window down, extended right arm
into up and down motion,
Otherwise, a shunt and one hell of a commotion.

Can you believe it? It's not that long ago,
Low powered engines, travelling so relatively slow.
Headlamp bulbs simple to replace,
Starting handles just in case.

*One Foot in the Grave

000 - 000

WELCOME TO BRITAIN

*"**L**et's move our shops out of town"*
So, into our cars we go on down.
"Cut our countryside transport services,
Reduce all urban speed to snails' paces."

"Ignore the growing list of deep pot holes,
And introduce inner city traffic tolls."
No vehicles will come a'calling,
Life and living will be quite appalling.

NHS is now DIY,
"You are number twenty-five".
Telephone queueing, so just sit and sigh,
Will I get to number one or die.

"Your prescription's ready to collect
And please show the 'desk' some respect"
The queue is long, she's multi-tasking,
So many questions the queue is asking.

Off with the form to the local pharmacy,
"Sorry today we can't fulfil this remedy.
Here's a few to see you through a day or two,
Come back tomorrow and join the queue."

And who will care for my old Ma?
A brilliant lass now a fading star.
Glamour is all the modern rage,
No desire to care for any old sage.

Defibrillators, wound packs, hang on public walls,
For all to use, no medics free to answer calls
The fist has been replaced by blade,
As hooded thugs wait in the evening shade.

Whilst continents keep emitting clouds of poison,
Pollution spreading across the whole horizon.
Experts meet for climate debates,
There'll be no food, no lights, cold kitchen grates.

"Let's plant trees, not corn nor wheat,
Import all the food we need to eat."
Self-dependence goes out through the door,
We'll all be in a mess come another war.

They've wasted money on false ideologies,
Not thought through and with no apologies.
It's political 'musical chairs', to dodge the blame,
And walk away displaying no shame.

000 - 000

TREE OF THE YEAR

A misty morning over my newly promoted city,
An old market town with history and identity.
Buildings that reflected days of business and trade,
Craftsmen's skill in brick and stone displayed.

Modern life now scorns this story,
Urban landscape no longer displays past glory.
Age has tarnished what we held with pride and dignity,
Permanency, durability not functionality
nor adaptability.

One feature of this community that's survived unscathed,
A five-hundred-year-old veteran tree, saved
From storms, disease, and German bombers overhead,
A sweet chestnut standing tall, edible nuts yearly shed.

Acton Hall, birthplace of the hanging Judge Jeffreys,
Demolished after World War Two with many park trees.
Not this old tree of lance shaped leaves, serrated edges,
Glossy dark green, all growing along its branches.

Like this old codger, life and time has left its mark,
Deep furrows and ridges developed on its bark.
Spiky cases protecting the nuts since those Roman years,
Early summer flowers from long upright catkins appears.

It stands twelve men high and twenty feet round,
And a few yards deep underground.
If trees could talk what tales they could tell,
Some folk residing in pomp, others living in hell

A sapling, planted at a time of slave ships arriving,
Of witchcraft, plague, and the Jacobite rising.
Handel's Messiah and Bonny Prince Charlie,
War with France and The Times out daily.

Then came the Act of Union – the United Kingdom,
Luddites, Robert Peel's police on the streets of London.
Factories Act reducing women and children's hours
of sweat,
Still accidents occurred with little employer regret.

There's more that this tree has encountered,
Storms and droughts stoutly weathered.
We all must be proud of this ancient tree,
IT'S THE UK'S TREE OF THE YEAR 2023.

000 - 000

Photographs supplied by

Wrexham County Borough Council.

ORDERING ON LINE

"**I**'ve found a useful piece of kit' she said,
"A plastic tool to help when making a bed".
"OK, send me an email with the site",
Modern communication, it doesn't seem right.

Checked my inbox, my wife has obliged,
Up comes the site, it's been well subscribed.
Placed an order, Oh! We get another one free,
Wasn't aware this item is made across the sea.

Order is acknowledged via sendgrit.net,
To track the package a link to activate.
This site is eight lines long of computer chat,
Tracking number has twenty digits, that's a fact.

Our item lies with Remo Inc. in the USA,
But awaits a carrier to get it on its way.
Ah! That's been sorted and it's off in transit,
To a Customs & Border Protection parcel unit.

The company kept me informed throughout,
And sent me a 'Best Regards' digital shout.
The item promptly arrived; plastic, cheap to buy,
Crossed a nation, across a wide ocean it did fly.

/over

Finger walking across each key,
Window shopping the modern way.
We purchased items made in GB,
Now from China and the USA.

Gone the Union Jack logos on our goods,
Just importing all, as we devour foreign foods.
By air, by land, and across many a sea,
We are ignoring the Global Warning plea.

I make no apology for this theme in my series' text,
Offered up on various pages in rhyming context.
I doubt I'll ever see the final outcome,
Action is needed now to save life and home.

000 - 000

THE SINS OF THE FATHERS *

Reflecting on my life and 20th Century living,
With periods of war and of mass killing.
Commenting on the life of our modern community,
I see confusion, a change of pace and of identity.

The actions of our forefathers are plain to see,
In Caribbean lands across the furthest sea.
On plantations of coffee and of tea,
Acquired by gun, abuse, and slavery.

It's left a mark, an ugly stain
For generations carrying their hurt and pain.
Their world was segregated by class and means,
Those who had full stomachs, those on beans.

We are faced with recognition of our obligation,
To give consideration for some reparation.
Confronted with the sins of our fathers,
Let's work together with our offspring
immigrant partners.
/over

Those so ignorant who think they are pure,
Should check their DNA percentage score.
We are a nation of mixed European blood,
Invaded with intent of doing no good.

So, lets develop this multi-cultural race,
With a soul, a heart, a future international place.
Seeking a life of achievement and leisure,
To work, to sing, to pray, in equal measure.

*Exodus 20:5

*Let him who is without sin,
Cast the first stone.*

John 8:7

PTSD AND TRIGEMINAL NEURALGIA *

Allow me this comparison of mental strain,
Each has a level of intense pain.
One is fallout from extreme past stress,
The other not knowing when there'll be more distress.

Both are stealthy and insidious affairs,
Unseen enemies creating fear and nervous flairs.
Result of modern conflicts for those who serve,
Or conflicts in the brain between artery and nerve.

One is the aftermath of violence and terror,
One not knowing the next facial furore.
Experiencing trauma on human life,
Death all around or pain from an invisible knife.

Is this twinge a nasal block
Or am I due for another shock?
Perhaps it's just a brief skin chafe,
Either way I'll play it safe.

Pop in a pill I carry around,
I don't wish to end up on the ground.
Not knowing if this is or isn't a foreboder
Of my traumatic stress disorder.

/over

Not knowing but ever expecting,
Constant stress and severe pain threatening.
Always alert, total embarrassment,
A constant trauma before the event.

PTSD is a recognised 'post pervader',
A mental and behavioural disorder.
TN's pre-trauma requires the same attention,
Greater awareness, understanding, and education.

*The author has also written about his encounter with
with Trigeminal Neuralgia in Book 5.

000 - 000

DEBRIEF ON BUTIN THE BADGER

Extract from a video filmed on 6 September 2024.

Regular visitor since circa 2018

DEBRIEF ON BUTIN THE BADGER

Readers of my books of rhyming poetry,
Will recall my nightly misery.
As Butin the Badger pays his regular calls,
Trotting around the lawn creating holes.

It's six years now since it all began,
And I no longer have a plan.
He's attacked from the East and the West,
Now from the South he's trying his best.

He's chewed through wood,
The wire fencing is no good.
That's been bent over to climb like an ape,
And digs underground like the Great Escape.

There's no chance of a peaceful settlement,
He's protected by laws of our British Government.
I'm sure he's full of bugs and fleas,
How far can he climb up trees?

He's a loner, big and strong,
Living rough, just getting along.
Around this area he makes his calls,
Our garden's one of his local Food Halls.

A life span of near twenty year,
Left his Set, perhaps in fear.
An immigrant seeking sanctuary here,
Should I open the gate, saying "Welcome Dear"?

LAY DOWN YOUR ARMS

Lay down your arms,
All you folk around the world,
Let the young ones all grow old.

Lay down your arms,
Take the road that has no violence,
And live a life of peace and silence.

Lay down your arms,
And save your skin,
Reunite with both your kith and kin.

Lay down your arms,
Love thy neighbour,
S/He could be your eventual saviour.

Lay down your arms,
Seek those of no ill intent,
A life of peace and total content.

Lay down your arms,
Throw off the clothes of war,
Nurse the sick and help the poor.
/over

Lay down your arms,
Don't follow like sheep,
Into an abyss so very deep.

Lay down your arms,
World leaders of evil intent,
Psychopaths with minds so warped and bent,

All you aggressive tyrants of murder and brutality.
Your life on earth promoting hate and cruelty,
Will surely end in death of the upmost
personal agony.

000 - 000

I HAVE BECOME AN AMAZONIAN

I have become an Amazonian for all to see,
Not a mythical woman warrior from near
the Black Sea.
But an old codger with a laptop and a cup of tea,
Dealing with the loss of shops near me.

I'm not armed with a club or sword,
Just the website and my acer keyboard.
I sit and scan this emporium in the sky,
Every item on earth is there to buy.

I don't have to wait in a queue,
In danger of COVID or winter flu.
Where items are scanned at a hell of a pace,
And looped musak played throughout the place.

I sit and shop in a sedentary style,
The ease of purchase just makes me smile.
It's not instant, just wait a day,
Brought to the door for no extra pay.

Soon my orders will arrive by drone,
As they whizz around the sky to the landing zone.
Day and night orders will be despatched,
Star gazers confused as new 'shooting stars' unlatched.

/over

Realistically, I've ordered an image from a screen,
Is the colour that shade of green?
Will the stitching itch my skin?
Will the fit make me look fat or thin?

There is nothing like handling the real thing,
For weight or shape and no misunderstanding.
But that opportunity for shopping is disappearing,
As Amazonians like me keep on ordering.

000 - 000

THE FACE

A friendly smile
Breaks mutual tension.
An invitation to stay awhile,
A visual tool of gentle persuasion.

Lips, that through them flow,
Uttered fast or meaningfully slow
Words of pleasure and of pain.
Sensual, tender, like delicate porcelain.

Eyes, the windows on your soul,
Reveals those inner feelings untold.
Brown, blue, green, or of grey.
Mesmerising, enchanting, and close to pray.

Ears, antennas listening out,
The slightest whisper, the loudest shout,
Stereo reception, perfect form.
Controls a body's balance to keep it norm.

The face is the mirror of the soul,
And a life-time story to behold.
Lines of age, of fun, of worry,
A reflection of one's personal history.

000 - 000

MY GENETIC CODE -2

Earlier I questioned my pedigree, *
My family history, my ancestry.
We must now travel from the Denbigh abode,
To part of the old Chester to Conwy Roman Road.

This is a story of abuse,
A roving predator on the loose.
A widowed farmer's untimely death,
His son, a loser left bereft.

I've mentioned my great, great, gran,
An illegitimate child named Ann.
Who was her father? pauper or squire,
No-one has ever dared to enquire.

Ann Hughes was her maiden name,
A pastry cook, confectioner of local fame.
To later marry David, farmer Williams' son,
A widower who did not then live long.

He took a new wife with two favoured sons,
When he died, his wife had the farm and all his funds.
His son David, destitute, a local chap brought up the lad,
A sweet, gentle, giant, rather 'dinewed' **, so sad.

*MY GENETIC CODE 1
** Harmless, naïve, simple, innocent

Ann was an entrepreneur, a business woman,
A farmer, hotelier, and a publican.
Who was her father, are these some of the clues?
An unlikely partnership for young Ms Hughes!

She took over the Rock Inn in old Lloc village,
Dressed all in leather an imposing image.
Hair she could sit on, with a head quite small,
Cared for by a maid, upon death, she inherited all.

Ann had just one son, Tom, who she sent away,
To train as a miller down the Liverpool way.
Stayed with Ann's cousins, millers by trade,
We know he succeeded and made the grade.

He returned to Wales, made Abergele his place,
Managed the mill, married an older girl called Alice.
He was a mandolin player of some renown,
Countless musical evening for folks of the town.

My Nain was a daughter of which there were four,***
A son, Philip, in the army who went off to war.
A happy family living at Pen y Bank all together,
Then the young went away, breaking the tether.

There are many questions on what went on in ages past,
Two irregular creations with parentages that did not last.
My genetic code will reflect the unintended intrusion,
My DNA may well offer up the personnel revelation.

*** Four daughters, two sons.

Ann Williams - Nain Rock from Lloc.

Tom Williams (centre) Miller

THE OLDER I GET

The older I get,
The better I used to be. *
But the older I get,
The more I fail to see.

It's names I forget,
Holding on daily to my cards and wallet.
It's taking longer for me to think,
Alas, my poor body continues to shrink.

I'm losing my taste for lager and beer,
And TV dialogue I'm failing to hear.
It's time to watch my daily diet,
And seek a life of peace and quiet.

The older I get,
I look back with little regret.
Blessed with a life of family joy,
A wife, three lovely daughters, one handsome boy.

Grandchildren ten in all,
Taking up the baton of life, all standing tall.
Great grandchildren have begun to arrive,
May they all from wickedness survive.

The older I get,
I think of all those I've met.
And the many still living in neglect,
The unbalance existing across this planet.

I cannot get much older,
So, I'll keep a watch over my shoulder.
You stay strong; look up, look far,
And may you all find your lucky star.

*John McEnroe's twist on
Mark Twain's 'The older I get, the more clearly
I remember things that never happened'.

000 - 000

MODERN WARFARE

A war with no boots on the ground,
Where man never fires a rifle round.
But sits in front of a digital screen,
In a room so spotlessly clean.

No trenches, no mud,
No witnessing death or spilt human blood.
Co-ordinates are set,
A button is pressed.

Right high up in the sky,
Armed drones and missiles fly.
Citizens below live in a state of fright,
As aircraft crew act to terminate their flight.

No-one has the right to maim and kill,
Destroy a life or seek ill
Of fellow man or his land,
Those leaders fail to understand.

This is no Xbox bedroom game for sure,
It's indiscriminate violence with evil intent.
By leaders of nations, destruction hellbent,
In power, but so immature, so insecure.

This modern world has no time, no place,
For those whose actions are a disgrace.
They rule by undemocratic means,
Creating pain and horrific scenes.

We are custodians of this planet constantly spinning,
Obliged to take good care of all things living.
Not plan to destroy land and all who reside thereon,
No modern society should accept such evil transgression.

000 - 000

FESTIVE THOUGHTS

As Advent season comes to an end
And Christmas cards made ready to send,
Eager expectations begin to grow,
Christmas shopping in stores all aglow.

The tree brought in and dressed, with love and care,
Baubles and lights, tinsel streams that glare.
The Christmas fairy, the Star of Bethlehem,
Atop the tree offering all a hearty welcome.

Homes are warmed as winter days begin,
But these days are short as night draws in.
'Old Faithful's' swamp our TV screens,
Reminders of those old Hollywood
kings and queens.

A host of cards have arrived by post,
Carrying greetings and news of the year now lost.
Prompting reflections of times spent together,
Of gatherings and holidays in all sorts of weather.

A quiet reflection stirs the heart and mind,
Of those who were helpful, caring, and kind.
Long since gone, leaving just a memory
To share, to ponder, a segment of our life's story.

Epiphany brings this short season to an end,
Annual prompting to send goodwill to family
and friend.
But goodwill is in short supply in our world today,
Violence stirred by religious beliefs holds sway.

How can 'Peace on Earth' have any standing,
As it lies on deaf ears just set on feuding.
For many this message is a common desire,
For others, love and tolerance are cast in the fire.

There are five predominant religions holding sway*
With differing beliefs, practices, having their say.
The Christmas message has a limited call,
But the sentiment of Christmas should be held by all.

*Christianity, Judaism, Islam, Buddhism, 4000 years old Hinduism.

000 - 000

FINAL REFLECTIONS

Generally, boys could always be seen
Wearing short trousers until aged thirteen.
Bruised and scarred knees regularly displayed,
Long length socks, family last for shoes repaired.

Meccano sets developing mechanical skills,
Radio Malt to fend off germs and ills.
Heat lumps and Calamine lotion,
Syrup of figs and mother's potions.

Pleasures were simple with little cost,
Communicated with far friends by post.
Our span of life in our world out of sight,
Just cinema's Newsreels in black and white.

Village cinema's Saturday matinee was quite a din,
The 'thruppenny rush' as we crowded in.
Hollywood films of Cowboys and Indians fighting,
Firing from horseback, always Indians dying.

Milk with cardboard tops drunk at morning break,
Those cardboard annular rings for pompoms to make
Classes nine to four, rote learning, very archaic,
We walked to school, no pain, no ache.

11+ examination divided the village's homegrown,
Those who remained, those who left for lessons in town.
Friendships lost; new friendships made with those from
elsewhere,
Village youth harmony fractured, difficult to repair.

Ballroom dancing, live bands playing,
Quick, and slow, close together romancing.
Then rock and roll, twist and shake,
Disc jockeys, turn tables, no refreshment break.

Chinese laundered starched white collars,
Shirt studs back and front, looking a million dollars.
'DA' hair style, 'Windsor' tie knot, family 'do's'
Drainpipe trousers, 'winkle picker' shoes.

Church and chapel formal weddings,
Ham salad, black forest gateau, sherry for toastings.
Semi-detached for two grand notes, quite appealing,
Full employment, new comprehensive schooling.

National Service stopped in Nineteen Sixty, *
Its intrusion to life and career such a pity.
But broadened young men into maturity,
New horizons, new friendships, and responsibility.

/over

How the 'Sixties "swung" and its fashion wear
I have written about it elsewhere.
Pop music, computer mouse, civil rights,
Moon walk, sliced bread, hideous tower block sights.

My reflections are too many all to share,
My wish has been to make you all aware.
Like antiques, memories become faint, then rare,
So, I have penned my odes and laid them bare.

I think I will just leave it there.

*Last conscripted men entered military service in 1960
and the last conscripts left in 1963.*

000 - 000

EPILOGUE

I make no apology for the theme of peace running through some of my poems in this book and my other books in the series. I came into this world just as the second world war was about to break out and throughout my life there have been countless wars, conflicts, murder, genocide, and unrest. As I have written in one of these poems, no-one seems to realise that we are just custodians of this planet. We do not own this land and its wealth. We should be working together to protect this planet and all forms of life.

It has been said that we all have a story to tell, a glimpse of how life has been for each one of us. Writing and publishing this final sixth book of reflective poems on my life and my observations on modern life, completes the mission I set myself six years ago. A true, personal, mirror on life in the 20th Century, and observations on how quickly life on this planet can change and is changing.

As Canadian physician Sir William Osler (1849-1919) suggested:

"We are here to add to life, not to get what we can from life"

....

THEY TRIED TO PUT THEIR TROUSERS ON STANDING UP!

EXTRACTS FROM BOOK ONE

THIS TINY ISLAND - 1
This tiny island so scarred and stained
By picks and shovels and muscles strained,
Deep in the bowels of this precious land
Men sweated and ached heaving coal by hand.

Dust in lungs, cuts in hand,
Scars on skin, wet clothes just hang
On bodies bent low swinging at coal,
Dynamite ready to shove in the hole.

THE TAID I NEVER KNEW
Miner John Robert Jones of Ffynnongroyw,
Made a move we all since rue.
He took my Nain and children too,
To the Welsh east border where coal seams grew.

He settled above the Alyn valley so steep,
To hew out coal two thousand feet deep,
At Gresford colliery across the green valley
Where near two thousand men had an underground tally.

WAR and BONDING
When I was two with a head full of curls
And milk teeth shining like a row of pearls,
Men with sons became men with guns,
And sons became guardians of their mums.

For many a night my mother and me
Sat by the radio after our tea,
We crept under the stairs when 'Gerry' flew past
To drop bombs on Liverpool with an almighty blast.

EXTRACTS FROM BOOK 2

OH! FOR A PERFECT WORLD
The recent 'Black Lives Matter' demonstration
Prompted deep memories of visiting one African nation.
Apartheid and life for those who don't fit in
With others who wish to dominate their pale skin.

Arrived in J'burg in '76 on a very sunny day,
Opened my suitcase in the room where I was to stay,
Everything was there except one thing I now needed,
The fundamental advice I had not heeded.

No sun cream to protect my soft Welsh skin,
I'll just pop out and buy a tube or even a tin.
A pharmacy was near-by and as I entered in
A large stand of skin whitening creams; was black a sin?

WHO OR WHAT IS A CELEBRITY?
'Celebrity' is bandied about,
But is it really worth a shout?
Let's take a moment to reflect
Who deserves to receive this epithet?

Is it one who saves a plastic football,
Or one who saves many lives each call?
Is it one who lip-syncs an adulterated song,
Or one who nurses patients all day long?

BREXIT DEBATE IN PARLIAMENT
Let's ask the people, the PM said,
The question's way above my head,
Do we leave or do we stay?
We will honour either way.

Oh dear! Oh dear! We are going to leave,
Let's vote again and vote Remain,
But that will be one apiece, I believe,
Oh dear! we'll have to go and vote again.

EXTRACTS FROM BOOK THREE

THE MIRACLE OF LIFE
As we witness the miracle of birth,
It is the greatest gift on earth,
A seed that swims to procreate
And life is born as it finds a mate.

With hair and toes and fingers too,
A face with nose, and eyes and ears two,
An early smile but that's just wind,
A heartfelt cry, she's a future Jenny Lind. *

WHO WOULD HAVE BELIEVED IT?
Who would have believed it?
Or even given credit,
That in the world we now live,
Change would now be quite so massive.

Supermarket trolleys like perambulators,
Personal details sold to advertising takers.
Year-long choice of all fruit and veg,
A plastic cup and a plastic peg!

POST-TRAUMATIC STRESS DISORDER
Military conflicts in years gone by
On land or sea or in the sky,
Approached in line abreast, colours held high,
Uniforms worn and battle cries.

The enemy was clear for all to see,
As comrades advanced, no doubt in fear.
A level of stress as battles abound,
Dead and injured lying all around.

EXTRACTS FROM BOOK FOUR

WORKING FROM HOME
'Working from home' is the new office dimension,
'Working at home' is to avoid any office tension,
'Working in the home' is a job with no pension,
Working at all is the new level of apprehension.

Attics have been cleared of forgotten gear,
That's hung around up there for many a year.
Flooring laid and stud walls constructed,
Ladders dropped down and wiring extended.

MY WARTIME CUISINE
As the enemy tried to starve our nation,
Attacking food conveys in the Atlantic Ocean.
Imported food and fruit were in short supply,
Rationing and 'Dig for Britain' was the cry.

Home grown potatoes, fruit, and local fish,
A housewife's challenge to create a dish.
The 'national loaf' of wholemeal bread,
Aided one's meal, it has to be said.

OUR PRESENT WORLD
I had hoped to reach a time in my life,
Sit back, relax with my dear old wife,
But our world is in such a state of strife,
Demonstrations, riots, and discontent so rife.

Violence is now too frequent on our streets,
iPhones to record and constant TV news repeats.
Racial abuse, female abuse, bullying, and rape,
Tormentors transmitting behind their I.T. cape.

EXTRACTS FROM BOOK FIVE

WHAT IS LOVE?
What is love which two living beings share,
And come together to form a pair.
Instant reaction, instant attraction,
Or a progressive friendship, a realisation.

A natural, comfortable, sense of bonding,
Absence triggering a heartfelt longing.
Amorous feeling, intense emotion,
A closeness that is more than affection.

ON-LINE SHOPPING
Enough of trolleys and checkout queues,
Of heavy bags and shopping 'blues'.
We'll do our orders all at home,
Delivered by van, but soon by drone!

The list is long, the freezer's low,
An on-line order needs to go
To that market emporium all aglow,
With stocks so high and prices low.

COAL MINES RESCUE TEAMS
Men of great courage and special grit,
When called, stepped forward to descend
their broken pit.
Never faulted, trained to rescue their fellow men,
Not knowing what was waiting in that deep black den.

A Rescue Team of Captain and six trained men
Stand prepared to do their job, accept their burden.
Find their friends trapped or lying down below,
The cage descends, the gates are opened slow.

The Author

Neil Davies is a Chartered Engineer, a member of two Engineering Institutions and the Royal Aeronautical Society. He holds the rank of Squadron Leader, serving sixteen years in the Education Branch of Royal Air Force. Late in his RAF career, he undertook a Defence Fellowship at UWIST Cardiff and was awarded the military symbol 'd.f'. for his work. Neil also has a M Sc in Applied Psychology. He subsequently held senior positions in Further Education colleges and came out of retirement on a one-year appointment as Principal and Chief Executive of a Yorkshire College to undertake and complete one of the first college mergers. Neil's responsibilities also included the provision of education services to four Yorkshire prisons.

At the age of 87, Neil has created a unique account of his life in the six books of rhyming poetry. Born in 1937, Neil grew up in the new model mining village of Llay on the outskirts of Wrexham during World War Two, enduring blackouts and rationing. Taking shelter under the stairs as German bombers flew overhead on their way to attack Merseyside. He has written poems on this period, and on through the 50's and 60's, the advent of the Beatles, to COVID-19 and LOCKDOWN.

Neil ends his fourth book with a poem written by his father whilst serving in the Royal Air force, stationed in the Naga Hills of Burma during World War Two. He also writes about his reaction when his father returns home from the war.

A church organist for over 35 years from the age of 17, Neil also includes a number of poems – 'Tales from the Organ Stool'. He has been married to his wife Joy for 64 years and they have four children, ten grandchildren and four greatgrandchildren.

He balances his reflective poems with his observational poems on modern life and global warning.